MOUNTAINS

A scene in the Sierra Nevadas of California   (Photo by C. William Harrison)

←A FIRST BOOK→

MOUNTAINS

Frances Smith

ILLUSTRATED WITH DRAWINGS AND PHOTOGRAPHS

FRANKLIN WATTS
London and New York

Franklin Watts Limited,
Chandos House,
32 Palmer Street,
London, S.W.1

CONTENTS

MOUNTAINS

These twisted layers of rock along the Red Deer River, Alberta, Canada, show how the earth's surface has bent in some areas   (Photo: The American Museum of Natural History)

EARTH'S MOUNTAINS

Mountains look as if they had been on the earth forever, solid and unchanging. Their appearance is far from the truth, however.

Mountains grow. They are born; they have youth, adulthood, and old age. They perish, and leave a flatness where they were. New mountains may rise from the roots of the old ones.

How can these things be?

The planet earth on which we are riding in orbit through space is a huge ball with a hot interior of less-than-solid minerals and rocks, and a cooler crust of rigid rock. Within the earth's interior, powerful forces are constantly at work, causing motion and change. Heat expands some areas of the earth; cooling may shrink others. Weights from the earth's surface press downward. The gravity of the moon and sun pull unevenly on the earth.

These disturbances, and others not yet fully understood by scientists, cause some areas of the rigid crust to move. Sections of the surface may bend or break or slip sideways. They may rise or fall. Great wrinkles of rock develop. The tops of these earth-wrinkles are our mountains, built up by all the invisible forces working on them.

But even as the mountains are being built, they are being torn down.

Surrounding the earth is the atmosphere, which contains many forms of moisture: clouds, rain, snow, ice. These things, too, are ever changing. Together with the heat of the sun, the push of the wind, and all the other elements of varying weather, they gradually wear away the mountains.

The building up and wearing down of the earth's mountains is unimaginably slow. In the billions of years of earth's life, mountain ranges in various places have come and gone, and come

1

Like other mountains, Mount Whitney, in California, is constantly being worn away by wind and weather (Spence Air Photos)

again. There have been long periods in earth's history when few high places existed and the land lay low and flat, with great oceans, lakes, and marshes over most of the surface.

The making of mountains is a vast puzzle that has not yet been entirely worked out. It is one part of the larger puzzle of the earth's beginning and its place in our universe. Scientists do not yet know exactly how our earth was formed. Formerly it was thought that the earth was a mass of hot rock and metal thrown off by the sun, and that as it whirled through space it cooled. It was thought that the cooling caused the surface to shrink into wrinkles, which were our mountains.

Many scientists no longer believe this is what happened. By observing the stars through powerful telescopes they have learned that our earth is only one small sphere in one small solar system in one galaxy. (A galaxy is a vast collection of thousands of millions of stars and other heavenly bodies which usually appear in a spiral, an oval, or an arc.) Our own galaxy, called the Milky Way, is but one in a sky full of galaxies. Perhaps our earth was formed about the same time as the stars, over four billion years ago. No one knows exactly how it was formed. Possibly it was a collection of particles, which during millions of years became fused together by motion and gravity. Even today many particles are pulled in from outer space by earth's gravity. They add hundreds of tons of weight to our planet each year.

THE EARTH'S INTERIOR

Although scientists do not know much about the earth's beginnings, they do know a great deal about what it is like today, on and immediately under its surface. By sending vibrations into the earth's interior and by tracing their courses, scientists have learned of the earth's composition. Long study of the rocks of the mountains has revealed many secrets for, in one way or another, these rocks have risen up from below the surface of the earth.

Earth scientists now believe that our planet is made up of three parts: the crust, the mantle, and the core.

Earth's *crust* is made up of rather brittle rock, and varies from about three to forty miles in thickness. Below this crust is the section called the *mantle*, about 1,800 miles thick. The rocks of the mantle are warmer than the crust, and more like a plastic of varying degrees from firm to soft. The *core* under the mantle is earth's very centre, altogether more than 2,000 miles thick. Many scientists believe that the earth's core is in two parts. The

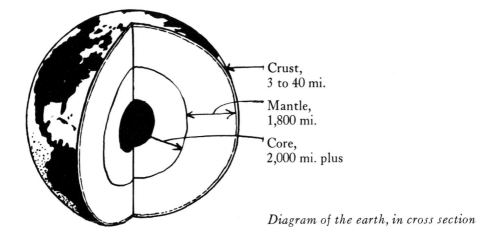

Diagram of the earth, in cross section

outer core — about 1,300 miles thick — is made of nickel and iron so hot it is in a molten, or liquid, state. The inner core is nickel and iron under so much pressure that it is solid.

To understand how mountains are made, we must always remember that our solid-seeming earth is actually a place of constant movement.

Our earth not only spins and orbits in space as a planet, but its interior rock shifts and moves. This rock trembles, and compresses, and inches its way back and forth and up and down. Mountains are made of material from the earth's crust, lifted and lowered by the interior motion.

What is the cause of the motion? Not all causes are known. Heat causes movement. This can be seen when water boils; or when a boiler goes on in a house and the rising hot air can be felt. Some scientists think that the interior heat of the earth sets up what are called *convection currents*. They create sideways pressure as they move through the rock of the mantle and crust. Radioactive atoms exist in certain interior rocks. This radioactivity can also set up movement. And even rocks or hard metal can be made to "flow" if enough pressure is put on them.

MOUNTAINS MADE BY FOLDING

The earth's various interior pressures act to build mountains in three ways. The first way is by folding. You can demonstrate this folding action by pressing the sides of a soft rug or a cloth so that it rises in ridges. Folded mountains are made in somewhat the same way. When heat, radioactivity, shifting weight, or other yet unknown forces within the earth's mantle exert pressure against certain areas of the earth's crust, the rock may arch or bend into folds. The best examples of folded mountains in the United States today are the Appalachians, near the Atlantic coast — especially the Alleghenies in Pennsylvania. From an aircraft these mountains appear as long lines of evenly spaced ridges, like the folds in a rug. In many other mountainous areas the folds are much more jumbled. Folds occur in rocks of various sizes. In many mountains where the bare rock shows on a cliff or slope, old folds

This cut along the bank of an old canal in Maryland shows folded layers of rock (Photo: U. S. Geological Survey)

can be seen. Sometimes small folds can be seen along a road where engineers have cut through rock to make the highway.

Of course there are differences between the folding in a rug and in a rock. Earth pressure is usually so slow and gradual that it is unnoticeable. Folding or arching goes on all the time, perhaps right under where you are sitting.

If folding is so slow it cannot be seen, how do we know it is happening?

There are places where movement can be measured over a period of years. Coastlines over the world have moved upward or downward and have left seamarks that show the changes. In Japan the remains of old campfires have been found forty feet below the sea. In many parts of the world the sea has carved caves which are now far above the highest tide.

The rocks of many folded mountains were once layers of sediment on the basin of some sea. How did they get from the sea to the mountaintops?

Scientists have some theories about this. They think it may have happened in this way. Water running down from the heights carries away soil, thus removing weight from the mountains, but adding it elsewhere to the earth's surface as sediment, especially in ocean basins along seacoasts. After a time the increasing weight of the sediment causes the area to sink deeper and deeper into the mantle in a downward curve. This curve is called a *geosyncline*, from the Greek word, *ge*, meaning "earth," and from two other Greek words meaning "to lean together." The layers of sediment are pressed together so hard that they become rock.

The bodies of sea creatures, particularly shellfish, also press into sediment. Because of the lime in the shells, these make layers of limestone.

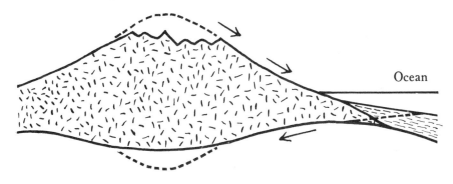

Ocean

Scientists think that sediments from the ocean floor may perhaps be pushed up into mountains in this way. Water running down a coastal mountain carries away soil, which finds its way to the ocean bottom as sediment. There the increasing weight causes the ocean bottom to sink. Then a sideways pressure may push underneath the nearby land mountains, causing the mountain-tops to rise, and pushing up new land, as well

The downward and outward bulging weights in the geosyncline exert a sideways pressure which may push in beneath the underground "roots" of adjacent mountains, causing the mountains to become heavier as their tops rise again. This change in weight may, along with other "squeeze" pressures, push the accumulated sediments back up into mountains. This seesaw effect is never exactly regular, and it takes place very, very slowly over many centuries.

It is important to remember that many other kinds of pressures, such as heat and energy currents, contribute to the slow seesaw effect. Some earth scientists believe that the shifting of weights may be related to the apparent balancing between whole continents and oceans. The rock of the continents is lighter in weight than the rock of the ocean basins. The continents may be "floating" on these denser rocks.

Mountain ranges seem to be only the top part of a particular mass of rock that extends beneath the surface of the earth's crust.

These theories seem to explain why there are so many folded

mountains that rise and sink along seacoasts. But all that is actually known is that, for the reasons given and others that are not understood, there are great shifts of weight in the earth's crust, and the shifts seem to work in rough, irregular rhythms over the ages.

One way of learning such things is by a plan called Project Mohole. This is an ambitious undertaking to drill right through the crust of the earth and into the rock of the mantle, and to bring up samples of the rock at varying depths. American scientists have used a type of oil well drilling rig mounted on a ship. The drilling has been done through the ocean floor, because beneath the oceans the crust is only about three miles thick. It is as much as forty miles thick in places under the continents.

Moho is the short name for the boundary between the crust and the mantle. (Its full name is Mohorovicic discontinuity.) Because earthquake waves travelling through the earth bend at this boundary, there is reason to believe that the mantle is of a different kind of rock from the crust.

MOUNTAINS MADE BY FAULTING

The second way mountains may be built is by faulting. Sometimes, instead of bending under pressure, as in folding, rock breaks. The break is along its weakest place. "Fault" is the word used to speak of a line of weakness in the crust. When pressure occurs at a fault, it may push the rock on one side of the fault upward as a block. It may shift the sides of the block in opposite directions. Sometimes it may also tilt the block so that one side of it has a steep slope and the other a gradual one.

8

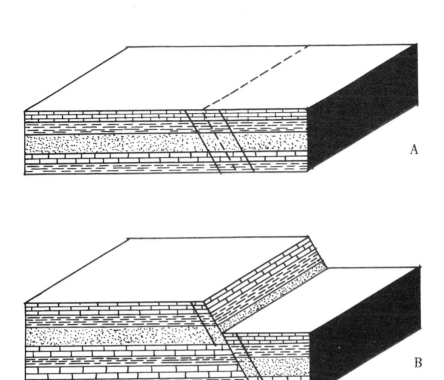

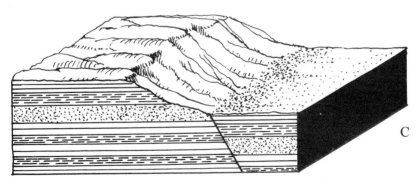

A fault in the earth's rock starts as a crack (A); pressure displaces the rock on one side of the fault (B); in time, the fault's sharp edges are worn away by weathering (C)

The Sierra Nevadas of today are fine examples of block mountains made by faulting. Near the Sierras in California are several lines of weakness. Tales told by Indians and passed down through the generations reported times when the land shook and split, when rocks crashed downward and the Indians fled for their lives. By studying the rock structure, geologists have learned what happened in the days of the Indian tales and long before. Originally a folded range, these mountains extended much farther east than they do today. Near the top of the range, north and south for many miles, a long break occurred. On the eastern side of the break a gigantic block began to split and slip away from the jagged peaks. This eastern block gradually sank lower and lower. It became the present-day Owens Valley. It left the western block as a long, sheer barrier of rock more than 5,000 feet higher than the valley.

Earthquakes are a violent evidence of movement in the earth's solid crust. In 1957 an earthquake in the Mongolian region of Asia

The Sierra Nevadas at Owens Valley have been split by a fault   (Spence Air Photos)

Anchorage, Alaska, in March, 1964. These buildings were situated precisely on a fault which became the centre of a violent earthquake. This section fell about 10 feet below the other side of the fault (World Wide Photos)

tumbled the tops of two 12,000-foot mountains into a narrow valley. The material from these mountaintops formed a new mountain 1,100 feet high. A mass of mountains 50 miles long rose as much as 20 feet, and moved about 10 feet to the eastward.

In March, 1964, the strongest earthquake ever recorded in North America occurred in southeastern Alaska. Underground stress caused the earth's crust to move in what is called a *slump* — some areas rose, others sank, along the coast from Valdez to Anchorage. At Valdez the land moved upward from 9 to 14 feet. Farther north at Whittier, it moved about 5 feet downward. In Anchorage, Alaska's largest city, some central streets were split to a width of about 12 feet. The quake created ocean waves that travelled through the sea to cause great damage as far away as California. Vast avalanches occurred in the mountains along the line of the quake. The energy released by all these earth movements was estimated to be more than a thousand times greater than the strongest nuclear bomb ever detonated.

11

Sometimes the action along faults is unnoticeably slow. Faulting can be the result of the same kind of interior pressures as those that cause folding. The difference is that the shift occurs along a line of weakness, and is a break rather than a bend. When, for a long time, pressures in opposite directions are put on the rocks in two adjoining sections of the crust, the rocks may bend slowly. Then suddenly the breaking point is reached and they rip apart along the line of the fault. This may happen in somewhat the way a cracked cup will break if pushed on from two sides, or from one side if the opposite one is against some immovable object.

Both folding and faulting in mountains are only the surface evidence of the deep, basic unrest within the earth. Another outward evidence of inner forces is what scientists call *volcanism*.

MOUNTAINS MADE BY VOLCANISM

Volcanus, or Vulcan, was the Roman god of fire, and patron of metallurgy. Volcanoes were said to be the chimneys of his underground smithies. From the time that ancient men first saw such fearsome explosions, they believed that the fire-breathing mountains were the home of gods or devils. The Indians of ancient Peru built temples in the very centre of the volcano El Misti, to quiet its angry spirit. Sometimes they even sacrificed human beings in an effort to keep the evil spirit from sending forth its deadly fire.

In the present era, most of the violent disturbances of the earth's surface seem to occur in certain "belts." Most active volcanoes are found within a belt called the "ring of fire." This belt circles the edges of the Pacific Ocean. Major earthquakes occur within this same belt. The ring of fire is obviously a place of great stress in the earth's interior.

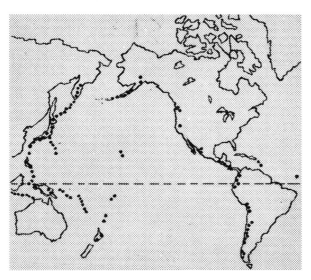

Most of the active volcanoes of the earth are found within a "ring of fire" encircling the Pacific Ocean

The material thrown out by a volcano is *magma,* or molten rock. Magma may be almost as thin as water or it may be as thick as mud, and it is lighter than the solid rocks around it. It rises through cracks, or vents, in the rocks of the crust. It spurts because it is usually mixed with gases. If you have ever pried the cap from a bottle of soda that has become warm, you know that the carbon dioxide gas in the bottle causes the soda water to spurt up like a fountain.

An *active* volcano is one in which the internal stresses may cause more or less frequent eruption. An *inactive* volcano is one in which the stress seems to have ceased for a long period. An *extinct* volcano is one in which the stress has completely ceased; sometimes all outward signs of volcanism have disappeared.

Usually it takes many volcanic eruptions to make a mountain, but sometimes the mountain is built rapidly. In 1943 a new volcano exploded in a Mexican field, and within a few years grew to 1,500 feet. That is about one-third the height of the famous

A volcano has an opening, leading from its underground reservoir of molten rock. The below-surface pressure of steam and gases sometimes causes the fluid rock to erupt through the opening as lava

Italian volcano, Vesuvius, which has been building slowly over hundreds of years. Mount Parícutin, the cornfield volcano, has now stopped growing — at least for a time.

Many volcanoes are beautiful, shapely mountains. Fujiyama, in Japan, is an almost perfect cone, sometimes capped with snow. So are Mount Hood, in Oregon, and Lassen Peak, in California. In Hawaii, beautiful Mauna Loa rises over 13,000 feet above ground level — over 30,000 feet from its base on the floor of the Pacific Ocean.

Mount Parícutin, in a Mexican cornfield, grew very rapidly within a few years after it first exploded (Photo: The American Museum of Natural History)

Fujiyama, in Japan, has the perfect cone of many volcanic mountains (Photo: Consulate General of Japan, New York)

Volcanic eruptions can be terrifying. Rocks, gases, cinders, and lava go hundreds of feet high. There is a wild red glow over the land. Friction may create electricity, making flashing lightning and rolling thunder. Rain may fall. Eruptions have sometimes buried entire towns.

These fascinating mountains are not all evil spirit, however. In

16

many parts of the world volcanic material, being rich in minerals and chemicals, forms valuable soil as the years go by. The wonderful crops of fruit and grasses in Hawaii owe much to volcanic soil.

We need to remember, however, that gradual movement in the earth's crust builds many more mountains than volcanism does. Folding is the chief cause of the major mountain ranges, but the folding process does not work alone. Folding, faulting, and volcanism often all occur in the same mountain area. The story the rocks tell is a complicated one.

HOW MOUNTAINS ARE WORN DOWN

No sooner do mountains begin to rise because of crustal movement than outward forces begin to wear them away, or *erode* them. The building up and the eroding go on at the same time. Mountain-making forces cause steep, uneven, sometimes jumbled surfaces, and most mountains grow so slowly that the eroding sometimes goes on faster than the mountain develops.

Old ranges like the Appalachian Mountains, now about 2,000 to 6,000 feet above sea level, have been uplifted and worn down at least three times. Anyone knows that dirt can be washed away by the force of a garden hose. The same thing can happen to rock. All through mountain areas, water carries cutting tools of sand and stone as it rolls downhill. Sometimes, in roadless mountain regions, streams are so swift that even packhorses cannot wade them, and travellers are forced to go far up or down

Mountain streams help wear away the rock of the earth's surface (*Photo by C. William Harrison*)

stream to a more level place that slows the current. Potholes many feet deep are sometimes worn in solid rock by tumbling water, and waterfalls cut the edges off cliffs.

Frost, too, is a rock breaker. It is composed of tiny ice crystals that expand as they freeze, enlarging any cracks in the rock. At last the rocks may break into pieces, even crumble into soil, some of which the wind blows away.

Wind and frost and all the changing weather are gradually wearing away the rock of these Arizona mountains (Photo: The American Museum of Natural History)

Seeds fall into bits of soil among the rocks. The roots grow and enlarge, pushing against the rocks. Chemicals from air and water and decaying plants also erode the rocks. Men, too, help wear away the mountains. Men cut lanes for electric lines. They build high dams. They build roads and trails. All these actions remove the rocks, soil, and trees from the earth's surface and create artificial channels for running water, for frost and ice, and quick-growing plants. Thus erosion is speeded up.

Sometimes on steep slopes the rocks loosened by erosion yield to gravity and roar down the mountain in a *rockslide*. Sometimes

This rock in Colorado is being pushed apart by a growing tree (Photo: The American Museum of Natural History)

Building roads like this one through the Saint Gotthard Pass in Switzerland has helped wear the land away   (Photo: Swiss National Tourist Office)

there is what looks like a river of rocks extending all the way down the slope, perilously resting, ready to slide more at any moment. At the foot of steep slopes there may be piles of rock and soil that spread out in the shape of a wide fan.

Glaciers are rivers of ice, which "flow" down mountains. They are formed when heavy snows accumulate on the heights and are pressed into ice. Like a giant arm with a clenched fist at its end, a glacier pushes rocks, pebbles, soil, and boulders as it goes.

20

Rock and soil, sliding down these mountains in Colorado, have formed great piles of debris at their bases (Photo: U. S. Geological Survey)

Cross section of a glacier, showing how its rocks and pebbles work to carve a U-shaped valley as they are pushed along by the ice

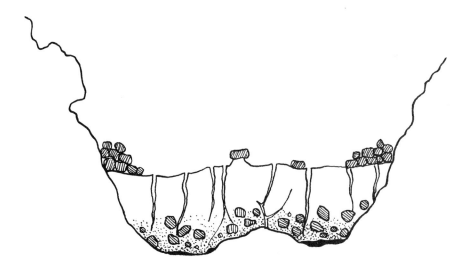

Untertheodul Glacier, in Switzerland, is a river of ice which pushes soil and rocks with it as it moves (Photo: The American Museum of Natural History)

These materials become fixed in the ice of the glacier at its sides, middle, and forward end. They act as mighty carving agents and cut a U-shaped valley down the mountain (a river cuts a V-shaped valley). Glaciers move at a rate of a few inches to a few feet a day in summer. When one flies over it, a mountain range with many glaciers looks like a mythical land of icy highways for giants.

The mountain rivers fed by meltwater from glaciers are milky white because of the rock dust ground up by the ice. After the rock dust has settled to the still water at the bottom, a lake may become a brilliant blue-green colour from the rock's chemicals and minerals.

Along some mountainous seacoasts, glaciers have cut steep-sided inlets called *fjords*. Norway, Alaska, Canada, Greenland, and New Zealand have many of these fjords. One of them in Nor-

An ancient glacier carved Colorado's Red Mountain Pass into its present U shape (Photo: U. S. Geological Survey)

way winds from the coast through cliffs and mountains for more than 100 miles to its head.

Everywhere in mountains the many forms of erosion have created magnificent scenery, sculptured by the varied forces of nature. On the rim of the magnificent Grand Canyon in Arizona there is a place named Inspiration Point. Many mountain points are called by this name, too, because the view inspires — it makes people aware of the wonder and beauty of our world.

All the lifting up and wearing down of land on the earth's crust proceeds with unimaginable slowness. Scientists can measure the age of any rock containing the radioactive element uranium. All uranium changes into lead, but at so slow a rate that 7,600,000,000

years would have gone by before one-half a given quantity had changed into lead. The age of uranium-bearing rock can be figured by comparing the amount of uranium in the rock with the amount of lead. From a study of many, many rocks, scientists believe the earth is *about* $4\frac{1}{2}$ thousand million years old. At the bottom of the Grand Canyon, more than a mile deep, there are some of the oldest rocks known to man—much more than a thousand million years old. They are only the roots of mountains which rose and were worn down over millions of years. If some magical clock could record earth's geologic time, the seventy-year lifetime of a person today would be only a tiny fraction of a second on that clock.

SOME GREAT MOUNTAIN RANGES OF TODAY

The Rocky Mountains are the greatest range of mountains in the United States today. They are part of a long chain stretching from the tip of South America all the way to the Arctic regions of Alaska. In the United States they extend from the Mexican to the Canadian border through the states of Arizona, New Mexico, Colorado, Utah, Nevada, Wyoming, Idaho, and Montana. Jagged and beautiful, they are a young mountain range geologically, but water, wind, and ice have sculptured them into bare peaks, ridges, and lovely deep canyons. They have slopes covered with majestic spruce and pine trees. They have broad, grassy valleys. The range is 3,000 miles long and up to 300 miles wide. In one state alone — Colorado — there are fifty-four peaks higher than 14,000 feet. The range's crest forms what is called the Continental Divide, the high point that divides the waters of the continent between two oceans. The melted snow and rainwater on the western slope run through hundreds of streams eventually to the Pacific Ocean, and on the eastern side to the Atlantic Ocean.

The hard rocks of the present Rockies were once part of a previous range of mountains. That range was levelled by erosion, and a sea came over the land some 500 million years ago. Sediments piled up 30,000 feet deep. Then a great squeeze began. From its pressures the Rockies were arched upward into high folds. The granite rock of the centre was lifted up. The covering of the granite was the sedimentary rock of sandstones, shales, and limestones from the sea. Erosion then washed away thousands of feet of the sedimentary rock. Other erosions and uplifts followed. Volcanic activity occurred here and there. Glaciers ground at the mountains. In all these ways the Rockies gained their present grandeur.

The splendour of the Rocky Mountains continues north of the border, where the range is known as the Canadian Rockies. They have no peaks as high as those in the United States, but they

The Rocky Mountains, looking south from Pike's Peak, Colorado (Photo: The American Museum of Natural History)

Mount Robson and Tumbling Glacier, British Columbia, Canada (Photo: Canadian Government Travel Bureau)

are beautifully sculptured and carry much snow on their tops. The highest peak, Mount Robson, is 12,972 feet. Masses of ice cover its steep slab faces. Great glaciers slip slowly down its sides. It makes its own terrible storms. In calmer moods it gleams in the suns of morning and evening with a shining, rosy light on its fresh snows. There are other wild and lonely mountains in the

Canadian Rockies, especially beautiful because of their snows and their many green-blue glaciated lakes.

The long system of the Rockies ends in Alaska in the Brooks Range north of the Arctic Circle. Mountains of the Brooks Range are not much more than 9,000 feet in altitude. Like the Canadian Rockies they are sheer and wild and lonely. There are no permanent inhabitants in the Brooks area except a few traders and trappers and a group of Eskimos who live in one of the passes. The mountains are the home of wildlife — caribou, bear, moose, wolves, and many small animals. The short, far-northern summer is beautiful in the forested valleys of the Brooks. The long winter is frigid and dark, but lovely, too, with snows gleaming on the peaks in moonlight and northern lights dancing in the sky.

Mexico, United States, Canada, and Alaska are lined with many beautiful high ranges all along the Pacific Coast. Some of these mountains possess jungles (in Mexico), some deserts (in Mexico and California). Farther north there are thick rain forests, deep fjords, and glaciers that drop huge icebergs into the sea. The glaciers are in northern Canada and Alaska, where there are coastal peaks as high as 19,000 feet.

The Alaska Range contains Mount McKinley, the highest mountain in North America. This massive mountain stands 20,320 feet above sea level and is 3,000 feet higher than its neighbouring peaks. It is one of the most splendid in the world because of its broad mass and its great blanket of snow. The Indians called it Denali, "the great one," and said it was the home of the sun. Here a large national park has been established, to safeguard its grandeur.

Part of the same chain as the Rockies, an even longer mountain system, the Andes, runs from end to end of South America. Its crest cuts through Argentina, Chile, Bolivia, Ecuador, Peru, Colombia, and Venezuela. The Andes were formed at about the

El Salvador Mine of the Andes Copper Mining Company is only one of many in the Andes Mountains   (Photo: Anaconda Company)

same time as the Rockies in North America. They are not yet even "middle-aged," as mountains go. Several parts of these mountains were created by volcanic action in the Pacific "ring of fire." The highest summit, Mount Aconcagua, about 22,834 feet, is an extinct volcano. Other parts of the system are the complex results of faulting, earthquakes, and the folding of sedimentary layers of rocks.

The Andes are rich in minerals; mining is important in all the countries they touch. Tin, copper, gold, and silver are among the minerals found.

The European Alps are undoubtedly the most picturesque and highly developed mountains in the world. They were formed in complex ways from folding and faulting, with folds that lapped

Mount Kilimanjaro looms on the horizon in the early morning light (Photo: Tanganyika Information Service)

over on other folds, and with areas of bedrock shifting sideways. These famous mountains have been studied for centuries by scientists, yet their puzzling structure has not yet been completely worked out in detail. They have been greatly eroded by water and glaciers. This erosion has carved sheer cliffs, horn-shaped peaks, deep valleys, and high slopes now full of grass and wild flowers in the summer.

Africa has no mountain chain that can compare with those of other continents. In the north of the continent the Atlas Mountains extend about 1,500 miles across Morocco, Algeria, and Tunisia. Their highest peak is the Toubkal, 13,665 feet. The mountains are formed of a rugged maze of high peaks, plateaus, and barren rock. There are smaller ranges and a few high peaks in other parts of Africa. Mount Kilimanjaro, in Tanganyika, and Mount Kenya, in Kenya, are the continent's loftiest mountains.

The name Himalaya means "Abode of Snow." Truly these Asian mountains hold their heads into the highest clouds. They are the highest of any continental range. The average altitude is 20,000 feet. Mount Everest, the tallest continental mountain in the world, is 29,028 feet — and still growing.

The entire Himalayan system is 1,600 miles long, and 100 to 150 miles wide. It consists of several parallel ranges in southern Asia in parts of India and Tibet. The ranges were thrust up originally by the violent crumpling of the earth's crust. Their rock shows that there were three definite periods of building, beginning in the north and working south. Here too is sedimentary rock from beneath an ancient sea. In some places, folds were pushed over on top of one another, and the bottom layers of rock became the top layers.

In the Alps, the beak-shaped Matterhorn rises above the valley village of Zermatt (Photo: Swiss National Tourist Office)

There are usually three seasons in the Himalaya: a cold season from October to February, a hot period from March to June, and a rainy season from June to September. The "rainy" season is a snow season in the high altitudes. Winds blow violently among the peaks. Here are probably the most forbidding, but most magnificent, of all the earth's mountain regions.

The mightiest mountain system in the world is not on the continents, but under the sea. It is 40,000 miles long and runs almost twice around the world. In places it is a thousand miles wide. Its total area is as great as Europe, Asia, and Africa combined. This long chain, made up of various mountain ranges, is called the Mid-Ocean Ridge.

Parts of the Mid-Atlantic Ridge, running in a north-south direction between the Arctic and the Antarctic, were discovered when a telegraphic cable was being laid across the Atlantic Ocean in the nineteenth century. Another section, the East Pacific Rise, was charted in a few places when ships cruising off the coast of South America detected very shallow places next to very deep places.

There are some strange things about these invisible mountain ranges. The Mid-Atlantic Ridge is split far down the middle by a long, long rift. One part of this rift can be seen in the North Atlantic Ocean where the top of the ridge rises above the water to become the island of Iceland. The rift can be seen there as a deep, narrow chasm. Another puzzling thing is that there are crossrifts, particularly in the mid-Pacific. This area is undoubtedly the scene of special violence in the earth's interior. Volcanoes and earthquakes occur on the ocean floor. Clever scientific detective work has been needed to learn about the mazes of marine mountains, their peaks, trenches, and rifts.

In one research method, TNT is dropped overboard from a laboratory ship, creating a small earthquake. The course and

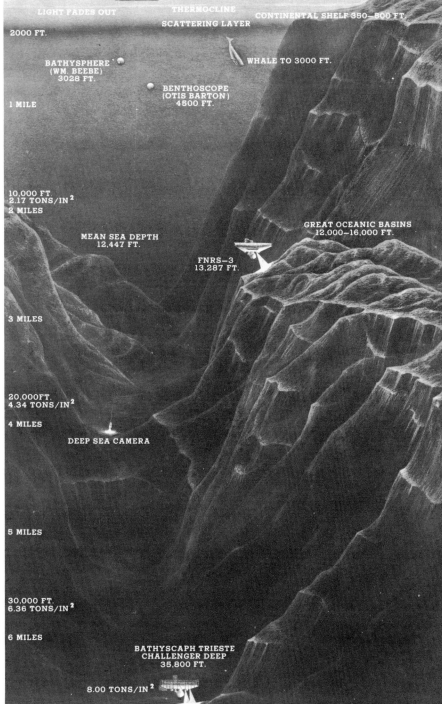

LIGHT FADES OUT

THERMOCLINE

CONTINENTAL SHELF 350–600 FT.

SCATTERING LAYER

2000 FT.

BATHYSPHERE
(WM. BEEBE)
3028 FT.

WHALE TO 3000 FT.

BENTHOSCOPE
(OTIS BARTON)
4500 FT.

1 MILE

10,000 FT.
2.17 TONS/IN^2
2 MILES

MEAN SEA DEPTH
12,447 FT.

GREAT OCEANIC BASINS
12,000–16,000 FT.

FNRS–3
13,287 FT.

3 MILES

20,000 FT.
4.34 TONS/IN^2

4 MILES

DEEP SEA CAMERA

5 MILES

*An artist's drawing
of the mountainous
ocean deeps and the
vessels that have
descended into them
(Official photograph,
U. S. Navy)*

30,000 FT.
6.36 TONS/IN^2

6 MILES

BATHYSCAPH TRIESTE
CHALLENGER DEEP
35,800 FT.

8.00 TONS/IN^2

depth of the quake's shock waves can then be measured on recording machines. In another method, echoes are bounced off the sea floor with sonic (sound) devices.

Nuclear submarines, cruising beneath the surface, have done some of the research work. When the U. S. submarine *Skate* made her first underwater voyage to the North Pole in 1959, she cruised across the top of the Lomonosov Range in the Arctic Ocean. Although the crewmen could not see the mountains, the lines made by the echo recorder showed them to be as jagged as the Rockies. *Skate's* commander, James Calvert, said: "We spent the night and the next morning zigzagging over the backbone of the range. . . . the fathometer needle drew dramatic profiles of soaring crags and spectacular valleys as they passed beneath us."

To explore marine troughs and canyons, other scientists have descended several miles into the ocean deeps in a special deep-sea craft called a bathyscaph.

A new type of craft is the Aluminaut, 50 feet long, which uses the most successful features of submarine and bathyscaph. It can cruise three miles down at about four miles an hour for several days. It has windows, floodlights, and cameras for still, movie, and TV pictures. This unique vessel and others will lift the mantle of invisibility from our fascinating marine mountains.

At the poles of the world there are mountains almost as little known as those beneath the sea. In Antarctica, several rugged ranges thrust rocky tops above the covering of ice. Mount Tyree, one of the highest on the frigid continent, lifts a massive ridge of bare rock at 16,290 feet. It is one of the mostly buried Sentinel Mountains of the Ellsworth Highlands, formed within the past 50 million years by the folding and upthrust of sediments. There is at least one active volcano, Mount Erebus, at the end of a long chain of dead volcanoes along the coast of Antarctica.

Greenland, the big Arctic island, is almost entirely covered by

The bathyscaph, Trieste II, *ready for launching at San Diego, California (Official photograph, U. S. Navy)*

the north polar ice sheet. Peaks rise here and there at elevations of 10,000 feet. All but their heads are buried in solid ice.

MOUNTAINS, CLIMATE, AND LIFE

If it were possible for a person to walk from southern Mexico northward all the way through the United States and Canada to the Arctic Ocean, he would start in a steaming jungle and end on an ice pack. He would pass through many changes of climate on the way. In each climate he would find certain kinds of plants and animals. Scientists have studied these climate belts and their special plants and animals. They have classified them into seven *life zones.*

At the Equator, the sun's rays shine almost straight down on the earth. Northward from the Equator the climate gradually grows cooler because the sun's rays strike the surfaces of the ball-shaped earth at a greater and greater slant, with less concentration of heat. In southern Mexico there is a hot, damp climate with jungles and swamps. This is the *tropical* life zone. In northern

Mexico and southwestern United States is a semidesert, or *hot-arid* life zone. If a person continued to follow the flatlands through the United States, he would find grasslands and broadleaf trees and a moderate climate. This is the *transition* zone between the hot and the cool climates.

Farther and farther north and into Canada, there are fewer broadleaf trees, and many thick stands of evergreen trees. This is called the *Canadian* zone. Still farther northward, the trees grow smaller and smaller and fewer and fewer as a person comes into the *Hudsonian* zone (named for the Hudson Bay area of central Canada). At last he passes out of the tree belt altogether and comes into the true *Arctic* zone where no trees grow, except occasional tiny ones that may look like vines creeping along the ground.

A person can see most of these same life zones simply by going up a fairly high mountain. The higher he goes, the cooler it becomes. In mountains it is not only latitude — distance from the Equator — which causes the increasing cold. It is altitude, or distance above sea level. Our earth's atmosphere is an ocean of air. The higher we move upward toward its top, the less air pressure there is, just as there is less water pressing on a diver in the upper parts of the sea than at the bottom. As air pressure lessens, the air expands and becomes cooler.

Each mountain life zone in each hemisphere has its own characteristic plants and animals, which may vary from continent to continent.

The natural plant and animal communities, or neighbourhoods, in life zones are not bounded by fixed lines. Obviously, between the neighbourhoods there is no fence like that surrounding a farm or an airport. There are no signs saying: "Snakes not permitted beyond this line." Yet there certainly are many more snakes in the lower, warmer regions than in the upper areas. And there is

36

Desert plants, southwestern United States   (Photo by C. William Harrison)

an altitude above which no snake will be found because the temperatures are too low for its cold blood.

In arid, hot lands will be seen those animals that have developed ability to live with little moisture. For example, in the southwestern United States cactus plants grow. Each segment of a plant is contained in a hard, waxy cover that resists evaporation. Sagebrush and some other plants have roots that run deep down, and light-coloured grey-green leaves that reflect the heat. There are ground squirrels, mice, badgers, and other animals that can burrow into the ground to escape the heat. The lizards and snakes have tough skins to protect them against the drying power of the sun.

A little higher, in either the Sierra or the southern Rockies, the *hot-arid* zone merges into the *transition* zone. Here are broadleaf trees, shrubs, and flowers. Here are deer, mountain lions, tree squirrels, rabbits, and other common animals and plants of the temperate zone. Another few thousand feet higher, and a person is among evergreen trees — pine, spruce, and fir. Here are found much the same plants seen in southern Canada. At last, in the highest regions, is the *Arctic-Alpine* zone, which is almost exactly like the far-northern tundra, except for the steepness of the land. And even here, of course, not every surface is steep. Throughout most mountains, even near the top, there are meadows, bowls, shelves, benches, saddles, and shoulders. Such words really describe the land shapes so named.

In the Arctic-Alpine zone of the Rocky Mountains there are wonderful examples of the way plants have become fitted to the surroundings in which they live.

The extreme heights are the harshest places in the mountain world. Winds may blow at more than 100 miles an hour; temperatures may fall far below zero in winter. Even in summer the thin air loses its sun-heat rapidly during the night. But life survives in this difficult world. Perhaps a seed falls behind a rock and takes root there where it is protected from the wind. If it grows higher than its shelter, winter wind and frost will probably kill the top part. Therefore most plants are not very tall. They take root in any place they can, but they creep over the ground, or grow sometimes in the shape of a cushion. In winter they simply become inactive and cease to grow.

A plant two inches high may send its root as far down as two feet. The deep root helps hold it against the pulling power of wind, frost, and erosion. Some plants grow together in clumps with a wiry mass of roots that is hard to pull out of the soil.

Snow is a protector. Tiny air spaces in snow make it an insula-

Bear grass in a forest clearing, Olympic Mountains, Washington (Photo: The American Museum of Natural History)

tor, just as the fluffy fibre glass used to insulate the walls of a house is. A plant or a mouse is safer beneath a snowbank than it would be on bare ground where there would be freezing followed by thawing, and where there would be lower temperatures and more wind.

Plants grow wherever growth is possible. Those plants which manage to survive are likely to pass on their qualities to their descendants. Suppose two pine trees are in two spots which are much alike. One pine happens to have a stiff, woody stock, and the other is more pliant. The stiff one will probably break off in the wind, and die. The pliant one will bend with the wind and manage to survive, and some of the pines that come from its seeds will inherit its characteristics. In the same way, the individual plants that happen to have the strongest roots will live, and some of the plants that grow from their seeds will also have strong roots.

Other plants may happen to be suited to use their inner foods and fluids slowly, so that they can last out a long winter. This

39

This mountain tree, bent and misshapen by the wind, has still managed to survive (Photo: The American Museum of Natural History)

ability may be passed along, too. So, over the years, many kinds of hardy plants have developed, while the weaker ones have died out. Some alpine plants have developed waxy leaves and petals that help hold moisture. Some have hairy surfaces that help hold heat. Because dark colours generally absorb more heat than light colours do, leaves of alpine plants are usually deep green; some remain green all winter. A few alpine flowers have dark inner surfaces.

The snow buttercup has been found blooming under as much as ten feet of snow. It has a way of using its food and fluids so slowly that it may lie almost lifeless during the winter, then may burst into bloom. In the high mountains, the willow may look like a vine, but it is really a tree. It has dense roots and a mass of tough little branches that lie flat along the ground. Lichens grow on bare rocks where nothing else can. In summer and autumn

The edelweiss grows far up on the rocky crags of the Swiss Alps. Like many plants of the high mountains, it is covered with woolly hairs, which help to conserve its moisture (Photo: Swiss National Tourist Office)

these tiny growths, fractions of an inch high, turn brilliant red or yellow.

Some animals, too, have been successful in meeting the hard conditions of the colder zones. The marmot, related to the lowland woodchuck of the United States, is famous for its high, clear whistle, which sounds as if it were made by a human being. It can be heard as much as a mile away in the thin mountain air.

The pika is about six to eight inches long, and although it is

The marmot's whistle can be heard for long distances in the thin mountain air (Photo: The American Museum of Natural History)

related to a rabbit, it looks more like a guinea pig. It may live even above timberline. During the summer it works busily at cutting grass and other plants with its sharp teeth. It places this "hay" in piles among the rocks. Then, in a snug underground den with its supply of food nearby, it goes through the winter on a high standard of mountain living.

Voles, or meadow mice, live all winter under the snow, making tunnels that lead to clumps of plants which furnish food.

The snowshoe rabbit is found at almost any altitude up to timberline. It gets its name from its ability to walk on top of the snow on its large feet, which have thick hair between the toes. The fur of this rabbit is brown in summer when the earth is brown, and white in winter when there is snow. This protective coloration makes the rabbit less easily seen by wolves, foxes, mountain lions, and other larger animals that prey on the rabbit population.

In the Rocky Mountain regions, mountain goats are the only large animals that live all year round in the stormy zones above the tree line. There, on places where the wind sweeps away the snow, they find enough plants to feed on. Mountain goats have four stomachs, and thorough digestion enables them to get every possible bit of nourishment from the twigs and leaves they eat. These wonderful animals have developed sharp-edged hoofs with "heels" that are almost like rubber. They can keep their footing on rocks and cliffs where nothing else can cling.

Bighorn sheep live on the heights in summer and move to the lower gorges and meadows in winter. The rams are noted for their curling horns, which sometimes grow in a complete circle. These sheep are much larger than the domestic kind, and they have long, straight hair instead of kinky wool.

Mountain lions are shy, secretive creatures that live in rocky dens in the middle or lower altitudes of mountain regions. They occasionally kill a rancher's calves or sheep, but this usually happens only when they cannot find their natural prey. Their value probably outweighs the little damage they do.

Many deer and bear are found in mountain areas.

Butterflies, bees, mosquitoes, spiders, and insects of various kinds are found in the mountains in spring and summer. They survive the cold nights of the heights because they simply stop moving. The coolness paralyzes them, but next day the sun warms them and they fly close to the ground. A few are caught in the strong winds and are blown even up to the snowfields.

The kinds of birds that can soar, or ride the updraughts of air currents over mountains, are eagles, hawks, swifts, and condors. During the winter most birds migrate to easier climates, but a few remain among the forested altitudes. The water ouzel (about the size of a sparrow) is the champion diver of the bird world. Even when the temperature is far below zero, it will dive into

Mountain lions inhabit rocky dens in the high country   (Photo by C. William Harrison)

mountain streams that flow so fast they do not freeze, and will come up with a bit of food. Apparently it has an ability to hover in running water.

MEN OF THE MOUNTAINS

Throughout the ages, mountains have been important in the lives of men. Mountains have influenced the course of wars. They have made men wealthy or held them in poverty. Mountains have caused separate forms of language to develop. Mountain passes and canyons have channelled the migrations of peoples for trade

The California condor, a mountain bird, sometimes has a wingspread of nine feet (Photo by C. William Harrison)

or conquest. In all these and other ways, mountains have affected the lives of men and of nations.

Why has this been so?

First, because mountains are barriers.

When a person climbs, the invisible force of gravity tries to pull him back. He has to move more slowly and breathe harder than he would on level land. Then too there are such dangers as rock- or snowslides, violent storms, and extreme temperatures. There are streams so swift and deep they cannot be crossed; they may flow through canyons impossible to bridge. These things are not so bad for a strong individual, but when large groups of people move and try to take their possessions with them, the difficulties are multiplied. Yet people have made homes in the moun-

45

tains. Sometimes men have entered mountain regions in order to seek gold and silver. Most often, in history, people have gone into the mountains seeking refuge from enemies, and have remained there.

Do mountains make their inhabitants different from other people? Are there life zones for men as there are for plants and animals?

No, not in the same way. It is true, the air at certain altitudes is so thin that even natives of the region cannot get enough oxygen to live. In 1963 the highest settlement in the world was in the Chilean Andes. There, in a tin mine at 18,000 feet of elevation, the Indian employees worked during the day, but descended to 17,500 feet to sleep. In 1960-61 a scientific expedition led by Sir Edmund Hillary in the Himalaya spent the winter at 19,000 feet. But most of the world's mountain people dwell little higher than 14,000 feet, and many live at lower elevations.

The mountains of the world rise in all latitudes and climates. The surrounding lands may have any degree of civilization from the most advanced to the most primitive. We cannot say that there is one typical mountain people. Geographers and others who have studied mountain people agree, however, that certain characteristics are likely to be found in almost any mountain region that has been settled a long time.

Patience and industry. Mountain people are likely to have these traits because farming, herding — in fact, daily life itself — all require hard, hard work on the steep slopes.

Acceptance of a low or at least a simple standard of living. Mountains yield their riches slowly. It is almost impossible to accumulate surplus cash. Education has been poor because it is so difficult to build schools and so hard for children to travel far to attend them. It takes all the labour of men, women, and children just to get enough to live simply. (Capital for investment in

46

In Switzerland, winter weather can isolate a mountain hamlet such as this (Photo: Swiss National Tourist Office)

mountain resources like mines and power dams comes almost always from men who have made their money in less difficult regions.)

Mountain people have been slow to change their ways. In valleys walled about by cliffs and peaks, communication with the outside world has been slow to develop. New ideas have taken a long time to penetrate the isolation. Mountain people have tended to live just as their ancestors did.

Religion and superstition are deeply felt, but are sometimes confused. In places where nature has been often violent, it has seemed to the people that there must be spirits and demons caus-

47

A devil dancer of Tibet takes part in a religious rite (Photo: Ewing Galloway)

ing the storms, the rock- and snowslides, the disaster, and the sudden death.

Self-reliance. Because of their isolation, mountain people have learned to depend on their own efforts for almost everything in their lives.

Special physical qualities. The high-altitude Andean Indians and the natives of the Himalaya have bodies that are short and compact, so that their blood does not have as far to circulate as in taller people. (The red blood cells contain hemoglobin, which absorbs the oxygen that the lungs inhale, and so helps carry it throughout the body.) Their lungs are large and can make the greatest use of the small amounts of oxygen in the thin air of the

48

high mountains. These peoples have grown into this helpful relationship with their surroundings over many generations — because they lived at such extremely high altitudes. The changes have made it possible for them to withstand low temperatures and thin air.

The difficulties of mountain living have shaped the lives of the inhabitants. But, in turn, the people have shaped the mountains. Man is not like other animals. He not only adapts to his surroundings, but he also changes his environment and tries to dominate it.

PEOPLE OF THE HIMALAYA

The boundaries of several countries run through the main ranges of the Himalaya — India, Kashmir, Bhutan, Nepal, Tibet, Sikkim, and to the west, Pakistan. Nepal has an area of about 54,000 square miles. It is an independent nation squeezed between India and Tibet, with Mount Everest, the highest of continental mountains, towering on its Tibetan border. Bhutan, even smaller, is semi-independent, under the protection of India. Vast Tibet, to the north, was independent for many centuries until 1951, when it was invaded by Communist China. Tibet is a plateau averaging 14,000 feet (this is higher than most of the Rocky Mountain Range). Many peaks in the Himalaya on Tibet's southern border rise above 25,000 feet. On the western flank of the Himalaya are the Karakoram Mountains, mostly in West Pakistan. Once the Karakoram held six small ancient nations with the delightful names of Swat, Dil, Chitral, Gilgit, Nagar, and Hunza. This region is an example of the way mountains have influenced the course of history.

49

In the seventh century A.D., followers of the Muslim faith invaded Pakistan and killed off most of the followers of Buddha. However — they did not enter the region of the Karakoram because the monasteries were so high up in the mountains and so hard to get to. The Muslim influence was held off from the six small nations for seven hundred years. Then at last it seeped in, but under much less violent conditions than formerly.

Even though the people of the Karakoram are now Muslims and most of the people of the other Himalayan ranges are of either the Buddhist or Hindu faith, all are deeply religious. The daily lives of those who live in the high villages or on isolated farms are alike in other ways, too.

With only the power of muscular arms and backs for farming and herding, the mountain dwellers have built terraces to make small fields. They have levelled off narrow strips on the steep sides of the heights, piling rocks into retaining walls to keep the soil from washing away. Some slopes are so thickly terraced that the whole mountainside looks like a series of steps for giants. Terraces are found in almost every inhabited mountain region of the world.

Mountain soil is usually thin and rocky. Men and women have to carry great bags of fertilizer — manure from their sheep and other animals — up to the fields. They have to carry the crops down in great baskets on their backs. Even with terracing, relatively few acres can be farmed. In Ladakh, an Indian state, only one acre in ten can be cultivated. In the Karakoram every bit of land is terraced, up to 10,000 feet. Yet there is often a food shortage. The average family there has only one sheep a year to eat. Cash income has averaged little more than £2 a year. In other Himalayan regions conditions are better than this, however.

Barley is the chief crop of the Himalaya, with some millet and

These Tibetan natives carry prayer umbrellas, used with appropriate chants in the fields at harvesttime to insure a prosperous season. The umbrellas are adorned with charms (Photo: Ewing Galloway)

potatoes. There is grass for animals. The Sherpas of Nepal pasture their yaks as high as 18,000 feet in summer.

The yak represents one of the best examples of the many ways which the men of the Himalaya have found to use what the mountains offered. The yak was originally a wild ox, a native to the heights. This long-haired animal was domesticated long ago, and now provides meat, milk, wool, hides, and transport. Even the tails are used. They are cut off and sold, to be used as fans in Asia and for Santa Claus beards in western nations. Yak butter furnishes the important fat needed in the diet in cold regions. Wool from the yak is spun into yarn on hand spindles and woven into cloth on looms.

These yaks form a caravan for transporting goods through the Tibetan mountain passes   (Photo: Ewing Galloway)

With minor differences, the high-altitude homes of the various nations are similar. The house is often built of stone and mud, on a steep, treeless slope. Any land that is relatively level is reserved for fields. A few houses have been built on places so steep that the buildings have had to be anchored to the mountain with chains.

In Tibet and Nepal the house is likely to be two storeys high. The lower floor is reserved for the animals. The people enter the house through this stable in which there may be sheep, goats, a few pigs or chickens, and yaks. Entrance to the second floor is up a narrow stair, or steps notched into a log.

The second floor is often only one large single room or a large room with a few closetlike rooms opening from it. There are usually no windows, for glass is scarce and the lack of openings helps to keep out the blasts of cold, violent wind. Cooking and heating are provided in a small stone fireplace. There is no chimney. A hole in the roof lets out the smoke — or some of it.

Cooking in Tibet is simple. A special brew of tea is likely to be both drink and food. It is usually made in a churn, a narrow cylinder with a plunger in it. Water is put into the cylinder, together with yak butter. These are thoroughly mixed by pushing the plunger up and down. Then the mix is brought to a boil over the fire. Tea is added, and sometimes a little barley meal. This makes a nourishing drink. To go with the tea, there are cakes of barley meal baked on a stone or flat pan, and sometimes there is meat. The fuel used in the treeless regions is dried yak dung, cleaned by rain and sun until it consists principally of dried grass, which burns with a hot flame.

In the simplest homes there are no tables or chairs, and beds are simple, made from yak and sheep hides. In Buddhist homes there is also a tiny room or corner set aside for a religious shrine, with a small lamp burning yak butter as a devotional. There are many Buddhist monasteries, sometimes built several storeys high on almost vertical mountainsides. Here the priests, or lamas, live. Yet, in spite of their religious devotion, many mountain inhabitants still believe that there are demons and spirits in the heights.

Warm clothes are needed. Men wear thick, heavy trousers and long coats with wide belts. Women wear long, heavy skirts and coats of wool. Felt hats decorated with charms to keep away the evil spirits are popular in some regions. Knitted caps with earflaps are worn in cold weather.

Until recently there were no wheeled vehicles anywhere in Tibet or the higher regions of Nepal. Travellers to Tibet in 1959 told of seeing men carrying disassembled parts of cars and jeeps on their backs, to be put together after they reached the Tibetan capital of Lhasa, hundreds of miles away. The Chinese are now

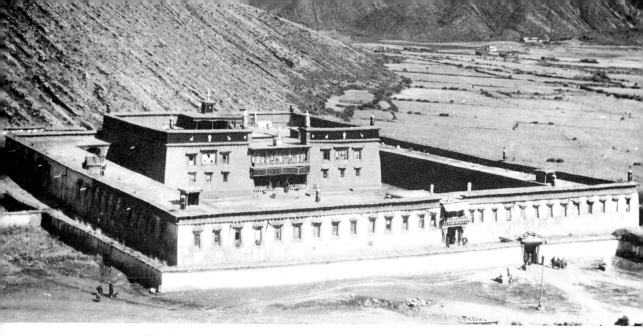

The Gelugba Monastery at Gartok, hemmed in by mountains, is typical of many such institutions in remote corners of Tibet. The building in the centre is a temple. The monks live in cloistered cells around the wall   (Photo: Ewing Galloway)

building roads in Tibet. India is building roads in her own country and helping to build them in Nepal, Bhutan, Sikkim, and the Karakoram. But it is a slow business. Today, and for centuries before this, trade caravans have wound over the passes, at elevations up to 17,000 feet, carrying wool and a few other products to the markets, mostly in India. Mules, ponies, and often sheep are the burden bearers. Men and women, too, carry great loads on their backs. When the market town is reached, trading is completed within a few days, then the long journey home begins.

In spite of the difficulty of their lives, the Himalayan mountain dwellers are a cheerful, pleasant people. They break the monotony of their lives by social gatherings around the fire and the drinking of tea or native beer.

54

A Tibetan woman shelters her child in her roomy sheepskin coat. Like many other women of Tibet, she wears her hair braided into 108 separate strands (Photo: Three Lions)

THE ANDEAN INDIANS

The second great mountain region of the world is the Andes of South America. Basically, there are similarities in the way the people of the two regions have been influenced by mountains and have in turn put the mountains to their own use.

Yet there are differences. The Andean people are of American Indian origin. Most of them now live in the high elevations of Bolivia, Peru, and Ecuador, with lesser numbers in Venezuela, Colombia, and Chile. In the dim past their ancestors, the Inca Indians and other tribes, found that the high places could be defended against raiding tribes from the lowland jungles. Between about A.D. 1200 and A.D. 1500 the Inca Indians developed a high civilization in the heart of the Andes Mountains. In the sixteenth century, however, the Incas were conquered by invading Spaniards, who used guns and ruthlessness against arrows and simplicity. The Spanish conquerors put the Incas, who had previously enslaved some of their own enemies, into virtual slavery. The descendants of the Inca tribes became cheap labourers, and farmers of tiny plots of land.

Because a large part of the Andes is at or near the Equator, the cooler, high elevations are better for living than the lower. Large cities exist at altitudes of 12,000 feet. This is almost twice the height of the city of Denver, Colorado, known as the "mile-high city." Andean Indian villages and remote pastures exist up to 17,000 feet.

During the period of Inca civilization, the Indians learned to use the mountains in many ways. They terraced the steep sides. They developed a remarkable system of irrigation canals. They mined gold and silver and worked it into jewelry and other art forms. Using stone, the material the mountains gave them generously, they became magnificent builders. Without any such

Machu Picchu, ancient stronghold of the Incas   (Photo: Three Lions)

thing as concrete, they fitted together stone blocks from one to
six feet high. Some of their fortress and temple walls have with-
stood hundreds of earthquake shocks. Although they did not

develop wheeled vehicles, they built stone-paved roads as wide as 24 feet.

They domesticated the llama, an animal related to the camel, but without a hump. Llamas are still found throughout the high Andes and they are used almost in the same way they were by the Incas. Like the yak, they provide meat, hides, wool, and fuel. They are never led, ridden, or harnessed. The Indian guides them right, left, stop, or start by a system of sounds somewhat like hisses.

The Andean man or boy wears loose-fitting trousers and shirt. His outer garment is a short *poncho*, which is actually nothing but a small blanket with a slit in the middle so that it can be put on over his head. It is woven of wool, often in a striped design.

A woman or girl wears a loose blouse and several layers of long, full skirts, modelled after those adapted many years ago from the Spanish. A shawl is her outer garment. The headdress of both men and women varies according to the community and the taste. It may be a high-crowned hat of felt or straw, a shallow-crowned hat with a wide brim turned up in sun and down in rain, or a warm knitted cap with earflaps. In spite of mountain cold, almost everyone goes barefoot, or at the most wears sandals.

Here, as in the Himalaya, the village or farm house is simple. Built of stone or sun-dried mud, it is usually little more than a hut, with a dirt floor and no windows. There may be hammocks for beds, or merely piles of blankets and hides on the floor. The llamas, sheep, goats, pigs, and chickens live outside the door, but are sometimes brought into the house. There is no plumbing. The sun is the only sterilizer. Contagious diseases like tuberculosis and whooping cough are common. The death rate is high, especially among children. Some of the most unfortunate people chew coca leaves from the plant that produces the pain-killing drug, cocaine. Chewing these leaves provides temporary energy

Llamas graze on a high plateau in Bolivia   (Photo by Sawders, from Cushing)

The town council of a Bolivian village in the Andes Mountains   (Photo by Sawders, from Cushing)

and deadens the pain or discomfort of ill health and poor living conditions, but it also lessens the individual's mental alertness, and may be habit-forming.

Most Andean Indians are very poor. They may have a few small, terraced fields for corn, potatoes, and other vegetables. Many do own llamas, which are highly prized and well cared for. But many people work for low wages in the tin and silver mines or on the large ranches in the valleys. The two principal groups of

These Andean Quechua Indians live in a hut of stone, in wild, roadless country (Photo: Three Lions)

the highlands today are those called Quechuan (pronounced Ketchwahn), because they speak that language, and the Aymara. These Indians are poor not only because life in the high mountains is difficult, but also because they are a different race from the other inhabitants, and because they were a conquered people from whom land was taken centuries ago.

The present governments of the Andean nations (and also agencies of the United Nations) are trying to improve their living conditions. New houses are now being built with windows, toilets, and septic tanks. In Bolivia and some other nations, land reforms have been started. Some large estates have been broken up into smaller farms, and some of the mountain people have been allowed to move onto these, where land is more produc-

Andes Indians work their terraced fields   (Photo by Sawders, from Cushing)

tive. Schools are being built, and a number of children attend school until they are 11 or 12 years old. A few then go to the cities for secondary school, college or even university.

And, like mountain people everywhere, in spite of the hard living, poverty, and other problems, the people find enjoyment. They are fond of dancing and fiestas. They enjoy the society of their friends and neighbours. They live close to nature amid great beauty. The high official of a mountain village in Venezuela said to a visitor: "I have been outside many times, but I always return. We may not have cars or jukeboxes, but here a man lives close to the soil. That, señor, is where God meant him to be."

PEOPLE OF THE EUROPEAN ALPS

The Alpine people are different from those of the Himalaya and
the Andes. On the average, the Alps are only about half as high
as the Himalaya, but because they are in a more northerly latitude, their weather is severe in winter. And even more impor-
tantly, the Alps are near areas which have been favourable to the
development of high civilizations. On one side of the Alps is the
way of life of southern Europe, especially Italy, and on the other
side is the way of life of western Europe, especially Germany and
France. There are many passes through the Alps. All the time
Europe was bringing itself to its present high state of development, people were travelling back and forth through the mountains. Busy cities grew up on the plains near the ends of the passes,
in France, Italy, Austria, Switzerland, and Germany.

*Roads in Switzerland's
many mountain passes
connect that country
with the remainder of
Europe (Photo: Swiss
National Tourist Of-
fice)*

Two thousand years ago, armies carried the civilization of the Roman Empire westward and northward through these passes. Tradesmen brought prosperity to the cities. In Austria a chain of mountain fortresses held off the invading Turkish armies and kept Asian influences from western Europe.

As a result, today's Alpine inhabitants live in the heart of Europe's highly developed civilization. The villagers whose ancestors have lived in the Alps for centuries are no longer backward, as are inhabitants of more remote mountains in other parts of the world. They have good homes and good schools.

The Alps are probably the world's outstanding example of how men have learned to use the mountains. Many parts of the Alps are full of facilities for tourists — sightseers, skiers, and climbers. The native people produce fine handicrafts, and famous products such as cheese and milk from the dairy cows they herd on the heights. Farming and herding, the usual mountain industries, are still carried on in a customary way.

In a typical village in Switzerland's Alps, streets may be so narrow that modern buses scrape the sides of the buildings at some points. Along these streets, cows and goats are driven along the way to the high pastures in the spring. (The word *alp* means "a high mountain meadow.") The pastures are portioned out fairly among all the villagers in the valley. A herder may live in a hut on the heights all summer. There may be a cheesemaking hut in the pasture, also. In other fields, hay is cut for winter feed and carried down by the farmer and his wife or perhaps piled up to be brought down by sled in the first snows. In autumn, the herds go back to stables in the village. The villagers devote themselves to handicrafts and to serving the winter-sports tourists. Women weave cloth, make lace or embroidery. Men carve wooden figures and make furniture. The typical house, called a *chalet*, is built of wood. It has a steep-pitched roof with wide eaves. There

In the spring, the Swiss villagers drive their herds to the higher summer pastures (Photo: Swiss National Tourist Office)

is usually a gallery around the second floor, with views of the lovely mountains.

Forests are important in the Alps. They furnish firewood for the cold winters. The trees help to hold the soil on the mountainsides and so are a great aid in controlling floods and avalanches. Avalanches, slides of either snow or rock, are extremely dangerous in the well-populated Alps. From the slopes above timberline, gigantic masses of snow and boulders may come sliding down to crush houses and take lives. The people of Alpine regions have learned to plant forests in the paths of possible slides. The forests are scientifically managed so that new trees are planted to replace those that are cut for fuel and for furniture and buildings. In

65

This high mountain pasture in Switzerland is wonderfully peaceful and quiet (Photo: A. Steiner)

recent years, too, dams and barrier walls have been built to catch avalanches or divert them from the villages.

Alpine dwellers have learned to use the force of fast-falling mountain streams to develop electric power. This power runs the railways and industries in the Alpine regions, and in the valleys and adjoining flatlands, as well.

Switzerland's many dams help furnish electric power to the country (Photo: Swiss National Tourist Office)

CHANGES ARE COMING

All over the world, wherever there are mountains, there are pockets of people who have developed distinctive lives. In the Pyrenees Mountains between France and Spain the Basque people for generations kept their own customs, costumes, and languages, even though the mountains are only about 10,000 feet high and though the passes, rising only about 2,300 feet, have been the main highways between Spain and the rest of Europe.

In the United States in the Appalachian Mountains of North Carolina, Kentucky, and Tennessee, and in the Ozarks of Arkansas and Missouri, pockets of people settled and stayed while other pioneers went on west. Some words common in the English language three hundred years ago are still used there although they have been dropped by other Americans.

But mountain people will not continue much longer in isolation anywhere. Aircraft can leap in minutes or hours over the rocky barriers that once took weeks and months to cross. A four-wheel-drive vehicle can grind up a very steep incline. Earthmoving machines can chew great bites from a mountain. Men with explosives can blow away the side of an unscalable cliff to build a winding road up its face.

Roads, rails, and electric power — but most important — sanitation and schools are slowly beginning to spread to the people of the Himalaya, the Andes, and other isolated mountain pockets.

MOUNTAINEERING: A SCIENCE AND A SPORT

In modern times, mountain climbing, or mountaineering, has become a sport and a science. About two hundred years ago a

Swiss naturalist offered a prize to anyone who would reach the top of 15,771-foot-high Mont Blanc. Twenty-six years passed before the prize was won. Few people climbed just for fun until about the 1850's. Then came a sudden interest in mountaineering. Soon every high peak in the Alps had been climbed. Between then and now, Alaska's Mount McKinley (20,320 feet), Aconcagua (22,834 feet), highest in South America, and Asia's Mount Everest (29,028 feet), as well as many other of the world's giants, have been climbed a number of times. The men who made these climbs developed the techniques that are used today. Now many climbing expeditions are made for scientific purposes as well as for sport. Climbers have added to knowledge of weather, geology, botany, and physiology.

Technical climbing, whether on large or small mountains, must be done correctly to be safe. Here is an example of basic technique. Let's say three people are going to climb a mountain in the Rockies. They are members of a mountaineering club. They have carefully learned their skill from club instructors. They have practiced by climbing only small cliffs at first. They always climb in a group because they know it is dangerous to climb alone. The most skilful man acts as leader. He carries maps, a compass for showing direction, an altimeter for measuring altitude. Each person carries an ice axe in his hand and wears a pack on his back. The packs contain food, warm clothing, sleeping bags. Someone carries a tent and small camping stove, for this mountain is large enough so that the climbers need to camp near the top to be ready to start for the summit early in the morning.

When they reach the steep part of the climb they "rope up." The leader takes a coiled climbing rope, usually 120 feet long, from his shoulder. He ties one end around his waist with a knot that cannot slip. The second person ties the middle of the rope around his waist, and the third person ties himself into the end.

This climber is descending by the rappel *method. His doubled rope passes around a secure point of rock above. His descent is controlled by the friction of the rope on his shoulders and hips, as he "walks" down the cliff. (Photo: Swiss National Tourist Office)*

The leader studies the cliff and chooses a route. He must be sure that there are enough cracks in the rock face so that he can find handholds and toeholds all the way up. The leader climbs first, while the others wait. When he has climbed a little way, he takes a hammer and a piton from his belt and drives the piton into a crack in the rock. A piton is a specially made steel spike several inches long, with an eye on the end.

70

The leader fastens the rope to the piton by means of a snap ring through which the rope can run freely. If the leader should slip, his fall would be checked by the man below him, who would brace himself to stop the rope running through the snap ring and the piton. This bracing for a hold is called a belay. When the leader reaches a ledge wide enough for him to sit or stand on, he belays the man below. He braces himself with the rope around his shoulder or a point of rock, and calls for the second man to start climbing. By this alternate climbing and belaying, one at a time, the three advance up the rock faces.

When they reach ice and snow they strap spikes, called crampons, to the bottoms of their boots. Each carries his ice axe in such a way that if he should slip he could dig the point of the axe into the ice and stop his slide. If the ice slope is too steep and smooth for footholds, the climbers will cut tiny steps into the ice with the ice axes. At last they will come out on the summit of the mountain with a good feeling of accomplishment and a deep enjoyment of the mountain heights. If they are lucky enough to find an ideal day at the top, the air will be utterly transparent, the wind cool and fragrant, the sun's rays warm. Far below, they will see flower-covered meadows, and on the horizon other peaks sparkling with snow or rich with brown rocks against blue sky. There is an "other-world" quality, a strangeness, perhaps a tiny hint of what the first men on the moon may have felt.

Technical climbing using rope, pitons, and other equipment on difficult slopes cannot be done without special training, but nontechnical climbing can be enjoyed on safe slopes. Even the nontechnical climber who just hikes up should know something about his mountain, though. He should know how to take shelter or to turn back if storms arise, how to avoid the hazards of slides, and so on. Every kind of climber should understand mountains as well as love them.

71

Mountain climbers, proceeding up an icy slope (Photo: Swiss National Tourist Office)

MOUNTAINS AS LABORATORIES

Earth scientists have studied the rock formations in mountains over the world. They have studied the fossils found there. (A fossil is either the imprint or the skeleton of a plant, animal, fish, or reptile that became pressed into sediment thousands of years ago and was preserved in rock.) By adding together the information about rocks and fossils in many regions, scientists have learned the geologic history of the mountains, and the ancient seas and plains, as well. Mountains have told most of the story, because tilting and folding turned the rock layers over, one upon another, revealing what the earth movements had been.

Mountaintops provide places to study the stars and weather, as well as earth's history. The McMath Solar Telescope, largest in the world, is located at Kitt Peak National Observatory in Arizona. It is housed in a tube 500 feet long. Other famous observatories are located on Mount Palomar and Mount Wilson in California; in Australia; and on various mountains in Europe.

On the top of Mount Washington in New Hampshire, a government weather station has recorded the "worst weather in the nation." Winds of 100 miles an hour are fairly frequent. The world's record wind speed of 231 miles an hour was measured in one gust on April 12, 1934. Winter temperatures may sink to 30 or 40 degrees below zero. The information collected there and on other summits has been of much value not only for forecast, but also for the United States military forces in their studies of arctic conditions. This remarkable mountain, although only 6,288 feet high, can often produce weather just like that of the polar regions.

There are volcanic laboratories in Hawaii; glacier laboratories in Washington state, Alaska, Switzerland, New Zealand, and other places. In many parts of the world, men have established permanent or temporary scientific laboratories on mountaintops.

73

U. S. Weather Observatory atop Mount Washington, in New Hampshire (Photo by Dick Smith)

MOUNTAINS AND NATURAL RESOURCES

We have talked about the lure of precious metals in the mountains, but some of their other natural resources are far richer than gold and silver. One of the most valuable is the contribution that mountains make to the atmosphere and climate. The coastal ranges of the northwestern United States are a good example of the way mountains influence climate. From far out over the Pacific Ocean, masses of air laden with moisture move southwestward. When such an air mass reaches the coast of Washington it meets the Cascade Range. Two things happen. The air striking the base of the mountains has to go upward. The higher it goes, the thinner the atmosphere is. The rising air, therefore, expands and cools. If it cools rapidly it condenses into clouds, and then into rain or snow. The other thing happens when the upper part of the moist air mass strikes the summits of the mountains. This, too, causes cooling and condensing.

Air masses striking the base of a mountain rise, expanding and cooling as they go. The air, if it cools rapidly, condenses into clouds, and then into rain or snow. The clouds lose their moisture on the windward side of the mountains. The leeward side is much drier.

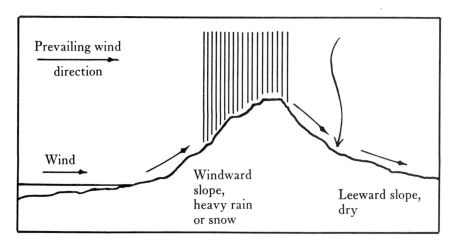

Prevailing wind direction

Wind

Windward slope, heavy rain or snow

Leeward slope, dry

In lush, green Hoh Rain Forest, Olympic National Park, Washington, the trees are draped with moss (Photo: Washington State Department of Commerce and Economic Development)

For these reasons the westward (seaward) side of the mountains sometimes gets 140 inches of precipitation (rain and snow) during a year. On the eastern side the rainfall is only about 12 inches, because the air masses have lost their moisture. On the seaward side, vegetation is so lush that ferns and hanging moss grow on the trees, which are hundreds of feet high. The ground cover of mosses, leaves, needles, and ferns is so moist and spongy that it will not burn. Forests of this kind are called rain forests. They are found also in Alaska, Africa, Asia, and South America, wherever mountains cause heavy rainfall.

Similar, though not so pronounced, differences in rainfall can be found between the western and eastern sides of Britain.

The variety of climate and terrain created by mountains is good for man because it keeps many kinds of life healthy and adaptable.

Mountains store water for the world. From high on the snowy summits come the streams and the underground water that make the valleys rich with food for the continents. Many great rivers of Europe rise in the Alps. There are the Rhine in Germany, the Danube in Austria, the Po in Italy, the Rhone in France. In America the Rockies produce the Missouri, Rio Grande, Colorado, and many other rivers. From the Himalaya come the Indus, Ganges, and hundreds of lesser streams. Rock dust containing chemicals and minerals is washed down, to make the lowland soil productive when stream waters spread over the fields by flooding or irrigation.

This valley in the Swiss Alps is fertile farming country (Photo: Switzerland Cheese Association, Inc.)

On the side of the mountain ranges away from the prevailing winds the air, having lost its moisture and upward surge, drops downward into thicker atmosphere. The land areas in this lee, or protected, side are arid. Yet in the dry valleys of interior California, Oregon, and Arizona, snow water held in the mountain heights is brought down to the dry land for irrigating orchards, gardens, and pastures.

The force of steep, falling streams is often harnessed by dams and dynamos to manufacture electricity, today's most valuable source of power for homes and factories over the world.

Sometimes, particularly in the western United States, arguments develop as to the proper distribution of the valuable resources of mountain areas. The slopes clothed with forests are wanted by lumbering interests. The slopes rich with grass are wanted by ranchers for their cattle and sheep. The water is needed by many different cities, farms, and states. If everybody selfishly took all he wanted, there would soon not be enough for anyone. Resources like trees, grass, and water can be used only in amounts that will be renewed naturally. If too much forest and grass is cut or grazed away from steep slopes, water runs down too fast. Floods result. Soil is washed away and the water wasted. So con-

These Swiss children are taken by their teacher to an outdoor class near a glacier (Photo: Gertrud Sta-hel)

These skiers in the Swiss Alps pause for a snack in the warm sun (Photo: Swiss National Tourist Office)

servation, or the wise management of renewable natural resources, is very important in mountain regions. Regulation of the conflicting interests constantly has to be worked out.

Many people now believe that the glorious scenery of mountains is also a valuable resource. They say that large dams should not be built in canyons or valleys that would better serve other needs.

And one of the greatest needs of all people is the need for recreation and for a chance to come close to the wonders of the natural world of which we are all a part. Mountains offer us this great resource.

Thousands of people go each year to mountain regions for fishing, hiking, camping, nature study, climbing, skiing, or just looking. They enjoy the clear air and the beauty. They feel the sense of mystery that mountains have always given man ever since the days when he thought them the homes of the gods. A feeling of wonder still flows into most people as they look upward at forested domes and ridges, at rocky cliffs and snowy peaks. It is then that they truly realize the natural miracle of all this grandeur thrust up, tilted, and carved by the age-old rhythmic movements of our restless planet earth.

Some Imperial & Metric Equivalents

1 ounce	28.350 grams
1 pound	453 grams
1 ton	1,016 kilograms
1 kilogram	2.2046 pounds
1 inch	2.54 centimetres
1 foot	0.3048 metre
1 yard	0.9144 metre
1 mile	1.6093 kilometres
1 metre	3.2808 feet
1 kilometre	0.6214 mile

INDEX

84

cooking and diet of, 51, 53
homes of, 52-53
occupations of, 50
physical characteristics of, 48
religion of, 50, 53
social life of, 54
superstition of, 53
Himalaya, the, 31-32, 46, 49-51, 54, 58, 68, 77
animal life of, 50, 51, 52, 54
crops of, 50-51
farming in, 50
height of, 46, 49
herding in, 50
plant life of, 50, 51
roads in, 54
soil of, 50
terracing in, 50
travel in, 53-54
Hindus, 50
Historic importance of mountains, 44-46
Horses, 54
Human habitation in mountains, 44-67, 68
adaptation to mountain conditions, 48, 68
characteristics of mountain people, 46-49
education, 46
farming, 46
herding, 46
mining, 46
occupations, 46
physical characteristics of mountain people, 48-49
religion, 47
see also Alpine people of Europe; Andean Indians; Himalaya, people of the
Hunza, 49

Iceland, 32
Inca Indians, 56, 58
India, 31, 49, 54
Indus River (India), 77
Inspiration Point (Grand Canyon), 23
Irrigation with snow water, 78
Italy, 63

Japan, 6, 14

Jungle, 35, 56

Karakoram Mountains (Himalaya), 49, 50, 54
Kashmir, 49
Kentucky, 68
Kenya, 30
Kitt Peak National Observatory (Arizona), 73

Ladakh (India), 50
Lamas (Buddhist priests), 53
Lassen Peak (volcano), 14
Lichens, 40
Life in the mountains; see Human habitation.
Life zones, mountain, 35-44
Arctic zone, 36
Arctic-Alpine zone, 38
Canadian zone, 36
hot-arid life zone, 36, 37
Hudsonian zone, 36
transition zone, 36, 37
tropical life zone, 35
Limestone, 6, 26
Lizards, 37
Llamas, 58, 60
Lomonosov Range, 34

Magma, 13
Marine mountains:
basic features of, 34
research conducted on, 33-35
Marmots, 41
Mauna Loa (volcano), 14
McMath Solar Telescope (Arizona), 73
Mexico, 14, 28, 35
new volcano (1943), 13
Mice, 37, 39
Mid-Atlantic Ridge, 32
Mid-Ocean Ridge, 32
Milk, 64
Millet, 50
Minerals, 29
Missouri, 68
Missouri River, 77

Mohorovicic discontinuity (Moho), 8
Mont Blanc, 69
Moose, 28
Mosquitoes, 43
Mount Aconcagua (volcano), 29, 69
Mountain climbing; *see* Mountaineering.
Mountaineering, 68-73
  clubs, 69
  enjoyment in, 71
  equipment needed for, 69-70
  history of, 69
  nontechnical climbing, 71
  scientific purposes of, 69
  technical climbing, 71
  techniques of, 69-71
Mountain goats, 43
Mountain laboratories, 73
  locations of, 73
  purpose of, 73
  types of, 73
Mountain life zones; *see* Life zones.
Mountain lions, 38, 42, 43
Mountain people; *see* Human habitation in
  mountains; Alpine people of Europe; Andean Indians; Himalaya, people of the
Mountains:
  climate, 32, 35-44
  composition of, 3-5, 6-7
  formation of, 1-2, 4
    by faulting, 8-12, 17
    by folding, 5-8, 17
    by volcanism, 12-17
  human habitation among, 44-68
  influence on climate, 75
  natural resources of, 29, 65, 75-81
  plants and animals of, 36-44
  recreation among, 68-71, 81
  scientific study of, 2-8, 10-11, 23, 25, 30, 32
  water sources, 6, 17-18, 22, 77-78
Mount Erebus, 34
Mount Everest, 49, 69
Mount Hood (volcano), 14
Mount Kenya, 30
Mount Kilimanjaro, 30

Mount McKinley, 28, 69
Mount Palomar Observatory (California), 73
Mount Paricutin; *see* Paricutin.
Mount Robson, 27
Mount Tyree, 34
Mount Washington Observatory (New Hamp-
  shire), 73
Mount Wilson Observatory (California), 73
Morocco, 30
Mules, 54
Muslims, 50

Nagar, 49
Natural resources in the mountains, 75-81
  grass, 78-79
  minerals, 29
  rivers, 65, 77
  trees, 77, 78
  water, 77, 78
  water power, 67, 78
Nepal, 49, 53, 54
New Zealand, 22
North America:
  earthquakes, 11
  fjords, 22
  mountain ranges, 5, 8, 17, 25-29
  volcanoes, 14, 26
North Carolina, 68
North Pole, 34
Norway, 22-23

Owens Valley, California, formation of, 10-11
Ozark Mountains, 68

Pacific Ocean, 12
Pakistan, 49
Paricutin (volcano), 14
Peru, 28
Pigs, 52, 58
Pika, 41-42
Piton, 70, 71
Plant life, 25, 30, 36-40
  adaptation to mountain conditions, 36, 38-
  40

86